# I'm sorry!

By Janine Amos

Illustrated by Annabel Spenceley

CHERRYTREE BOOKS

A Cherrytree Book

Designed and produced
by A S Publishing

First published 1998
by Cherrytree Press Ltd
a subsidiary of
The Chivers Company Ltd
Windsor Bridge Road
Bath BA2 3AX

*British Library Cataloguing in Publication Data*

Amos, Janine
    I'm sorry!. – (Good manners)
    1.Interpersonal relations – Juvenile literature
    I.Title II.Spenceley, Annabel
    395.1'22

ISBN 0 7540 9047 7

Printed and bound in Malaysia

# On the beach

Yasmin and Nimet are playing frisbee.

Nimet is running fast.

She does not look where she's going.

Nimet squashes the castle.

How does the little boy feel?

How does Nimet feel?
What could she do?

Nimet says sorry.

# Ouch!

Everyone's waiting in a line.

Carrie steps backwards on to Kim's foot.

Carrie is busy talking.
She does not say sorry.

How does Kim feel?

Carrie turns round.

How does Kim feel now?

# Late for the match

Daniel is waiting for his brother.
He is taking Daniel to the match.

Daniel waits for a long time.
He is cold.

At last Will rushes up.

How does Daniel feel?

Will thinks about it.

Will says sorry.

How does Daniel feel now?

31

"There are many different ways to hurt someone. You might bump into them. You might hurt their feelings in some way. You might spoil something of theirs by accident. Show you understand how they feel by saying I'm sorry."